MW00560456

# Contents

**CLASSIC FESTIVAL SOLOS** offer the advancing instrumental soloist an array of materials graded from easy to more challenging. An assortment of musical styles has been included to give variety and to allow an opportunity for the musician to develop interpretive skills.

**Jack Lamb, Editor**

© 1992 BELWIN-MILLS PUBLISHING CORP.
All Rights Assigned to and Controlled by ALFRED PUBLISHING CO., INC.
All Rights Reserved including Public Performance

# VENTURE

LEONARD B. SMITH
ASCAP

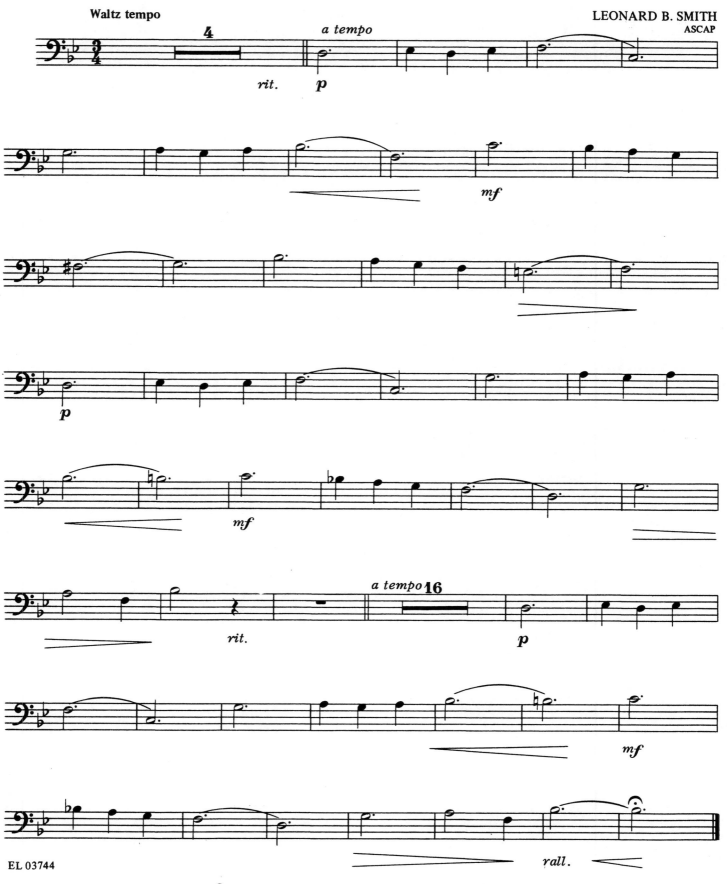

EL 03744

Copyright © 1973 by BELWIN MILLS, c/o CPP/BELWIN, INC., Miami, FL 33014
International Copyright Secured     Made In U.S.A.     All Rights Reserved

# LAZY LULLABY

DONALD C. LITTLE

EL 03744

Copyright © 1977 by BELWIN MILLS, c/o CPP/BELWIN, INC., Miami, FL 33014
International Copyright Secured     Made In U.S.A.     All Rights Reserved

# MILITARY MARCH

TRADITIONAL
Arranged by DONALD C. LITTLE

EL 03744

Copyright © 1977 by BELWIN MILLS, c/o CPP/BELWIN, INC., Miami, FL 33014
International Copyright Secured    Made In U.S.A.    All Rights Reserved

# WEATHER VANE

PAUL TANNER

EL 03744

Copyright © 1980 by BELWIN MILLS, c/o CPP/BELWIN, INC., Miami, FL 33014
International Copyright Secured      Made In U.S.A.      All Rights Reserved

*To Lou Cohen*

# DEBONAIR

LEONARD B. SMITH
ASCAP

EL 03744

Copyright © 1973 by BELWIN MILLS, c/o CPP/BELWIN, INC., Miami, FL 33014
International Copyright Secured     Made In U.S.A.     All Rights Reserved

# LAS TORTILLAS

PAUL TANNER

EL 03744

Copyright © 1980 by BELWIN MILLS, c/o CPP/BELWIN, INC., Miami, FL 33014
International Copyright Secured     Made In U.S.A.     All Rights Reserved

# SONG TO THE EVENING STAR

## From "Tannhäuser"

RICHARD WAGNER
*Arr. by Leonard B. Smith*

This is one of the most famous songs of all time. It requires attention to phrasing and to projection of tone. The term "eloquent" most aptly describes this music.  LBS

EL 03744

Copyright © 1965 by FIRST DIVISION PUBLISHING CORPORATION
Copyright Assigned 1968 to BELWIN MILLS, c/o CPP/BELWIN, INC., Miami, FL 33014
International Copyright Secured        Made In U.S.A.        All Rights Reserved

*To Rowena Fremont Platte*
# UNICORN

LEONARD B. SMITH
ASCAP

The term *"giocoso"*, a direction in music, is the key to the successful performance of this solo. It means *"lively, with jollity, playful"*. Note, too, the use of contrast in volume - the *f* and *P*; also the swells.    LBS

EL 03744

Copyright © 1970 by BELWIN MILLS, c/o CPP/BELWIN, INC., Miami, FL 33014
International Copyright Secured        Made In U.S.A.        All Rights Reserved

*To Clarence W. Chase*

# SENTINEL

LEONARD B. SMITH
ASCAP

EL 03744

Copyright © 1973 by BELWIN MILLS, c/o CPP/BELWIN, INC., Miami, FL 33014
International Copyright Secured      Made In U.S.A.      All Rights Reserved

For Walter Beeler

# LITTLE NORWAY

LEONARD B. SMITH
ASCAP

In this solo, the several *ritards* should be very slight, just enough to enable you to give a *"lilt"* to the piece. Each time your first three notes appear, they should be played with a *"bounce"*. Don't chop off the eighth note in measure 4 of your solo part, but glide to it gently. LBS

EL 03744

Copyright © 1970 by **BELWIN MILLS**, c/o CPP/BELWIN, INC., Miami, FL 33014
International Copyright Secured    Made In U.S.A.    All Rights Reserved

*For Ron and Kay Knudsen*

# CONCENTRATION

Allegretto moderato

LEONARD B. SMITH

You will probably observe that the piano accompaniment to this solo revolves around an eight measure sequence which occurs in different keys. Your melody line, however, changes continually and if you decide to play the solo from memory, you will require "Concentration".

L.B.S.

EL 03744

Copyright © 1965 by FIRST DIVISION PUBLISHING CORPORATION
Copyright Assigned 1968 to BELWIN MILLS, c/o CPP/BELWIN, INC., Miami, FL  33014
International Copyright Secured        Made In U.S.A.        All Rights Reserved

# GALAXY
## (Theme and Variations)

Maj. HERMAN VINCENT

EL 03744

Copyright © 1971 by BELWIN MILLS, c/o CPP/BELWIN, INC., Miami, Florida 33014
International Copyright Secured     Made In U.S.A.     All Rights Reserved

14

15

EL 03744

# GYPSY RONDO

J. F. HAYDN
Arr. by LEONARD B. SMITH

EL 03744

Copyright © 1973 by BELWIN MILLS, c/o CPP/BELWIN, INC., Miami, FL 33014
International Copyright Secured      Made In U.S.A.      All Rights Reserved